About Level Learning:
Level Learning provides a literacy focused
designed for K-12 Chinese as a Second L
Our program offers 20 levels of specific ar
leveled texts and passages, mastery-bas
and analytics to enable data-driven instru
reading curriculum for both literature a
emphasize grammar and comprehension
develop confident and independent Chin
The non-fiction series of books are
to support our informational text cours
national standards. To learn more about
www.levellearning.com.

About Washington Yu Ying PCS™:
Washington Yu Ying PCS is a Mandarin
immersion International Baccalaureate (
Ying's mission is to inspire and prepare y
a better world by challenging them to re
in a nurturing Chinese/English educ
Yu Ying's comprehensive IB, dual ir
equips students with global competer
the real world. As a leader in immersion
is determined to advance Chinese lang
global citizenry education by helping
and strengthen their Chinese programs.
email: products@washingtonyuying.org

考虑对方的感受

Social Emotional and Multicultural Learning |
Non-Fiction Series

Copyright © 2022 by Level Learni
Ying PCS™
Original and Edited Text Copyrigh
Ying PCS™

All rights reserved. No part of this
be reproduced without written per

Published by Level Learning, INC.
Content Contributors:
Washington Yu Ying PCS™
Level Learning - Ya-Ching Chang

Illustrations by: Josh Taira

Leveling classification based on L
For full description, visit www.leve

ISBN 978-1-64040-082-5
Simplified Chinese Edition

和别人交流的时候，要考虑对方的感受。我们要用别人可以接受的方式来交流。

比如，我看了一个同学的笔记。我对他说："你的字真难看，我都看不懂。"这样的话，会让他伤心。

我可以说:"你的字写得清楚一点会更好。"

比如，有个同学午餐吃饺子。我对他说："你的午餐真难闻。"这样讲没有礼貌。

我可以说:"你的午餐味道很特别。"

比如，一个同学回答完问题。我对她说：“你的声音太小了，我们都听不到！”这样说会让她失去信心。

我可以这样说:"你的声音大一点会更好。"

我们要诚实，同时也要考虑对方的感受。这样说话才不会伤害别人。

Glossary

	Pinyin	English Definition
别人	bié rén	other people
交流	jiāo liú	to communicate
考虑	kǎo lǜ	to consider
对方	duì fāng	other person, receiving party
感受	gǎn shòu	feeling
接受	jiē shòu	to accept
方式	fāng shì	method
比如	bǐ rú	for example
笔记	bǐ jì	notebook
说	shuō	to speak
看不懂	kàn bù dǒng	unable to make sense of what one is reading
会	huì	can, able
伤心	shāng xīn	to feel hurt
清楚	qīng chu	clear

	Pinyin	English Definition
午餐	wǔ cān	lunch
饺子	jiǎo zi	dumpling
难闻	nán wén	bad smell
礼貌	lǐ mào	courtesy
特别	tè bié	special
声音	shēng yīn	voice, sound
信心	xìn xīn	confidence
诚实	chéng shí	honest
伤害	shāng hài	to hurt

www.ingramcontent.com/pod-product-compliance
Lightning Source LLC
Chambersburg PA
CBHW041225070526
44584CB00001B/95